GO SNOWSHOEING!

by
Heather Bode

CAPSTONE PRESS
a capstone imprint

Published by Capstone Press, an imprint of Capstone
1710 Roe Crest Drive, North Mankato, Minnesota 56003
capstonepub.com

**Library of Congress Cataloging-in-Publication Data is available on
the Library of Congress website.**
ISBN: 9781666345957 (hardcover)
ISBN: 9781666345902 (paperback)
ISBN: 9781666345919 (ebook PDF)

Summary: Readers will learn about the proper clothing, footwear,
and supplies they need to go snowshoeing in the wild outdoors. They
can discover how to have fun while safely exploring the winter world
around them.

Image Credits
Alamy: ITAR-TASS News Agency, 9; Getty Images: Adam and Kev,
7, bauhaus1000, 5, Caroline Woodham, 10, Caroline Woodham, 22,
Jupiter Images, 17, 24, Manuela, 8, Ron Nickel, Cover; Shutterstock:
Albert Garrido, 21, Bruce MacQueen, 27, CCISUL, 23, ChiccoDodiFC,
14, Dan Thornberg, 13 (left), Debbie Galbraith, 15, EB Adventure
Photograpy, 18, Macrc Bruxelle, 1, marekuliasz, 13 (right, middle),
Maridav, 19, michelangeloop, 25, Michelle Baumbach, 29, Scott E
Read, 12

Editorial Credits
Editor: Erika L. Shores; Designer: Dina Her; Media Researchers:
Jo Miller and Pam Mitsakos; Production Specialist: Tori Abraham

All internet sites appearing in back matter were available and accurate
when this book was sent to press.

Printed and bound in the USA. PO4882

Table of Contents

Words in **bold** are in the glossary.

LET'S FLOAT!

What do you think of when you hear the word *floating*? Do you imagine yourself in outer space? Maybe you are in a swimming pool. There is a winter activity that can help you "float" on top of the deepest snow. What is it? Snowshoeing!

Snowshoeing is a great way to go hiking in winter. Snowshoes spread out a person's weight over a large area. This allows you to float on top of the snow instead of sinking into it.

Snowshoeing began in central Asia about 6,000 years ago. People living in other snowy areas also used snowshoes. The **Indigenous** people of North America depended on snowshoes to explore the continent. Today, snowshoes are used by the military, forest rangers, outdoor guides, mountaineers, and anyone who enjoys hiking.

Indigenous people wore snowshoes to hunt bison during
North American winters.

Chapter 1

GETTING OUTSIDE

Why do people snowshoe? It is easy to learn and inexpensive. People of all ages and abilities can snowshoe. You must be able to walk. You do not need to take lessons like you might with skiing. This lets you get outside quickly.

Snowshoeing provides exercise in winter. It is a good workout for your heart. At the same time, it is easy on your body because snow is a soft surface.

Being outside in winter, when there is not as much daylight, can help improve your mental health. Our bodies need vitamin D, which is produced when we are exposed to sunlight. Also, the crisp air helps clear our minds. This can help lift our moods.

Snowshoes make it easier to get outside and hike
during snowy winter months.

The Need for Vitamin D

In winter, most people do not get enough vitamin D because
they spend more time indoors. Our bodies make vitamin D by
combining sunlight with a chemical found in our skin. Some foods
like milk and cereal have vitamin D added to them. Vitamin D
helps our bones stay strong. It also helps muscles stay healthy and
keeps our brains functioning.

Snowshoes strap on to regular winter boots.

Snowshoes are available to rent from outdoor equipment stores. Renting your equipment will help ensure that you are wearing the proper size snowshoes. This also lets you try snowshoeing to see if you enjoy it!

Do you like to race? You might decide to try out snowshoe racing. The sport is becoming more popular. People wear special snowshoes that let them run. Running in snow is twice as hard as running on roads, while being gentler on your body. There are world championship snowshoe running races. Perhaps someday it will become an Olympic sport!

People who enjoy running and want to do it on snow may compete in snowshoe racing.

Snowshoeing is a fun activity for a family or a group of friends. It does not require a lot of special equipment. Most of what you need you may already have.

Snowshoeing is also a safe activity. You move at a slow and steady pace. Follow these tips:

☑ Don't snowshoe near water and ice. This will help you stay dry. It is also difficult to tell if the ice is thick enough to support your weight.

☑ Always snowshoe with a buddy. If you need help, someone is there.

☑ Check the weather forecast. Winter weather can change quickly.

☑ Dress for the weather. Your body needs to be protected from the cold.

☑ Apply sunscreen to your face. Sunlight reflecting off the snow can cause sunburn.

FACT

It is easier to think in the cold than in the heat. It takes less energy to keep your body warm than it does to cool it. That extra energy can be used by your brain to think!

Chapter 2

SNOWSHOE DESIGN

There are animals that travel over snow. Watching them probably provided inspiration for snowshoe design. Some snowshoes looked like the hind feet of snowshoe rabbits. Others looked more like bobcat paws.

A bobcat's wide paws help it move easily over deep snow.

Early snowshoes had a wooden frame, rawhide **decking**, and leather **bindings**. The decking is the flat area that connects the outer frame to the bindings. The bindings are where your boots attach to the snowshoe.

There were three main snowshoe shapes. The long Alaskan, or Yukon, measuring almost 4 feet (1.2 meters), was used to walk on deep powdery snow. The Huron, or beavertail, shaped like a tennis racquet, was used on all types of snow. The bearpaw design was short and oval. It did not have a tail like the other two types of snowshoes. It worked well in forests.

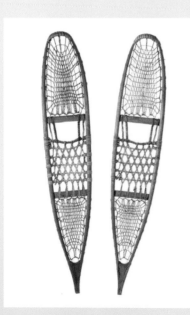

Alaskan or Yukon snowshoes

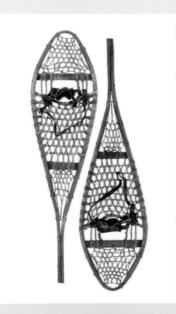

Huron or beavertail snowshoes

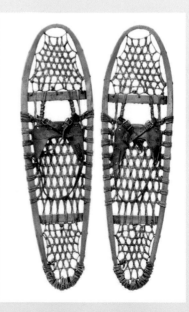

Bearpaw snowshoes

There were problems with early snowshoe designs. The wood broke and the leather bindings often snapped. They were heavy and hard to walk in because they were so big. Eventually, new products were invented, which helped improve snowshoes.

Most of today's snowshoes follow the Sherpa design. This is a smaller oval snowshoe with an aluminum frame. Aluminum is a metal that is lighter than wood. Plastic frames are also common. The decking and bindings are made of waterproof material to prevent cracks and breaks. Cleats, or **crampons**, run across the toe and sometimes the heel area, and provide better grip.

Metal crampons are located under the toe area of snowshoes.

Modern snowshoes are similar in design to the traditional bearpaw snowshoes.

Chapter 3

GET READY, GET SET, GO!

If you rent snowshoes, the store's workers will make sure you get the right size and style of snowshoe. The style depends on where you are snowshoeing. You can rent poles that look like hiking poles. They help you balance, but you can snowshoe without them.

Choosing where to snowshoe is easy. Start in your yard or neighborhood. This lets you get used to walking in snowshoes. Another place to snowshoe is where you like to hike in the summertime. You may be surprised how different the landscape looks in winter. You can snowshoe at local parks, on golf courses, or even on hills. Snowshoes let you explore wooded areas. Do you have a forest nearby? Check it out on snowshoes.

As long as there is enough snow, you can explore almost anywhere on snowshoes.

It's important to wear clothing that protects your body from getting cold and wet.

You can wear snow boots or waterproof hiking boots for snowshoeing. If you wear hiking boots, use **gaiters**. Gaiters cover the top of your hiking boots to help keep snow out of them.

Dress in layers. This allows you to add or take off clothes based on your body's temperature. You can wear long underwear, athletic pants, and snow pants. Bring a winter hat and gloves. Carry a small backpack to hold snacks and water. Pack an extra sweatshirt, hat, and gloves. Try to keep the backpack light. Remember that snowshoeing is a lot of exercise.

Snowshoers should bring a small backpack to carry supplies.

Snow Cones, Anyone?

Bring flavored gelatin packets on your trip. Be sure you use only fresh, clean snow! Sprinkle on the gelatin. Mix and enjoy a flavorful treat. You can also use maple syrup to make a snow cone. Bring paper cones, add snow, and drizzle the syrup on top.

Chapter 4

WALKING LIKE BIGFOOT

Before setting off on your adventure, find the left and right snowshoe. (Some snowshoes can be worn on either foot.) The buckles should be on the outside of your boots. Loosen the straps. Make sure your boots are secure on your feet.

Slide your boot into the strap openings. Stop when you feel the toe hinge under the ball of your foot. This is an opening toward the front of the snowshoe by the crampons. It allows your foot to move and will provide the most grip. Tighten the toe straps first. Then tighten the heel strap. Finally, tuck in any straps that may cause you to trip.

Be sure all snowshoe straps are tight
and secure on your boots.

Once your snowshoes are secure, start walking around to find your balance. Your feet have just gotten much bigger! You will have to take shorter and wider **strides**. The deeper the snow, the shorter your stride will be. You also need to lift your knees higher than you normally would while walking.

If you sink as you move, try packing the snow before stepping forward. Use your snowshoe to pat down the snow a few times before putting your weight on it.

Start out by taking small steps with your snowshoes.

Snowshoeing in a line allows the people behind the leader to walk in their tracks.

If you fall, roll over onto your stomach. Bring one knee forward so you are half-kneeling. Bring your other knee forward and stand up.

Take turns breaking the trail if you are snowshoeing in a group. The person in front "breaks" the trail by putting the first tracks there. This is the hardest job.

FACT

Snowshoes are meant to go forward only, not backward. To turn back, go forward and gradually turn around.

To snowshoe uphill, there are two ways you can move. For gradual slopes, use the **herringbone**. Point your toes out and the tails of your snowshoes in. The prints you leave will look like a duck's steps. If you face a steeper slope, you will want to **traverse** it. This means you walk in a zigzag pattern going up gradually instead of going straight up.

To go downhill, keep your weight centered over your snowshoes. Keep your knees slightly bent. If you are using poles, keep them in front of you to help you balance. Let your front crampons grip the snow to prevent sliding.

Snowshoers climb a hill using the herringbone method.

Going downhill, you'll bend your knees and use
your poles to balance.

Chapter 5

THE MAGIC OF SNOWSHOEING

Snowshoeing can be harmless to the environment because snow covers and protects it. The more snow there is, the higher you float above the ground. Stepping on plants or objects poking through the snow damages them. This can also damage your snowshoes. There should be at least 6 inches (15 centimeters) of snow on the ground for snowshoeing. This protects you and the environment.

Seeing wildlife in winter can be exciting. However, give animals plenty of space. We are visitors to their **habitat**. Do not leave food for them, even though you might think it is helpful. Animals need to be able to find their own food so they can survive once humans leave.

A quiet walk through the woods on snowshoes means
you may spot wildlife, such as white-tailed deer.

Snowshoeing is a simple, fun outdoor activity. You do need to keep a few rules in mind. They are:

☑ Do not use **groomed trails**. These are for skiers. Snowshoes can punch holes in groomed trails.

☑ If you come across other snowshoers, allow the ones moving downhill to go first. They are probably moving faster. Step aside and let them pass.

☑ If you find an object from nature, leave it there. Take a picture of it instead.

The real magic of snowshoeing has been the same for thousands of years. You float across the snow, and after a while the snow melts. There is no evidence you were ever there. Enjoy the memories of your adventure in the great outdoors!

Tracks in the snow made by snowshoes

GLOSSARY

binding (BYN-ding)—the part that attaches the boot to the snowshoe

crampon (KRAM-pahn)—a metal strip with jagged edges that look like sharp teeth or spikes

decking (DEK-ing)—the flat area of the snowshoe between the frame and the bindings

gaiter (GATE-ur)—a protective sleeve worn over a hiking boot that keeps snow out of them

groomed trail (GROOMD TRAIL)—packed-down snow created by a snowmobile pulling mechanical equipment

habitat (HAB-uh-tat)—the natural home of a plant or animal

herringbone (HAIR-ing-bohn)—a way to go up a slope by alternating angled steps with toes pointed outward

Indigenous (in-DI-juh-nuhss)—the first to live in a place

stride (STRIDE)—the steps you take

traverse (truh-VURS)—to travel back and forth across an area

READ MORE

Butler, Erin K. *Extreme Snow and Ice Sports.* North Mankato, MN: Capstone Press, 2018.

Gagliardi, Sue. *Get Outside in Winter.* Lake Elmo, MN: Focus Readers, 2019.

Van, R.L. *The Science of Snow Fun.* Minneapolis: ABDO, 2022.

INTERNET SITES

37 Snow Games and Activities: Outdoor Winter Fun
kidactivities.net/games-play-snow/

Winter Sports for Kids
activekids.com/winter-sports

INDEX

ABOUT THE AUTHOR

Heather Bode is an elementary educator and author. She loves writing nonfiction she knows will be high-interest material for her students. Heather lives in Helena, Montana.